INTRODUCTION

The *Rite of Christian Initiation of Adults* is the process by which adults become members of the Catholic Church. It can be described in terms of periods of learning and decision-making (inquiry or precatechumenate, catechumenate, purification and enlightenment, and mystagogy). The RCIA process can further be described in terms of the steps (inquirers, catechumens, the elect, neophytes) these adults pass through in their faith development. Each step is celebrated with a rite, a public worship ceremony, that marks the closure of one stage along their faith journey and a transition into the next step. In addition, there are ceremonies that occur within a particular step, for example, the scrutinies.

These rites bring home the point that the journey of faith is not so much a solitary journey as it is a journey guided by catechists—teachers of Catholicism—with the individual support of sponsors and the communal support of the whole parish and diocesan faith communities, indeed, ultimately with the support of the entire Catholic Church. This pamphlet explores, in an introductory manner, these rites of the RCIA.

SETTING THE STAGE

Those who have addressed a hunger for more knowledge about the faith—whether in answer to the communal work of evangelization or in answer to their own inner urges—and are ready to pursue serious "classes" in Catholicism, are also ready for the first official rite of the larger *Rite of Christian Initiation of Adults.* They are

LITURGICAL SIGNS & SYMBOLS

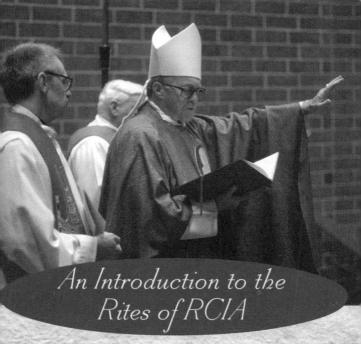

An Introduction to the Rites of RCIA

ELSIE HAINZ McGRATH

Imprimi Potest:
Richard Thibodeau, C.Ss.R.
Provincial, Denver Province, The Redemptorists

Imprimatur:
Most Reverend Timothy M. Dolan
Auxiliary Bishop, Archdiocese of St. Louis

ISBN 0-7648-0910-5 • © 2002, Liguori Publications
Printed in the United States of America
06 05 04 03 02   5 4 3 2 1

To order, call 1-800-325-9521
www.liguori.org
www.catholicbooksonline.com

Interior photographs by Bill Wittman

Elsie Hainz McGrath has an M.A. in Theology from Aquinas Institute of Graduate Theology, Saint Louis, and has been involved in parish RCIA ministry for fifteen years. She is a Senior Editor at Liguori Publications.

ready to move from an unofficial state called the "precatechumenate" or period of inquiry into the local parish catechumenate program. This is often the first time many parishioners are aware of who these people are. It is their opportunity to be a welcoming community, for they will be asked to accept these aspirants to Catholicism as catechumens or candidates for full communion.

This pamphlet addresses itself primarily to "catechumens," meaning those who have not been baptized. The *Rite of Christian Initiation of Adults* is also adapted for "candidates," however—those who are baptized but wish to be received into full communion into the (Roman) Catholic Church. All Christian baptisms are valid and unrepeatable; baptism is a once-for-always sacrament. Often, therefore, there are more candidates in RCIA programs than there are catechumens because of situations where parents have had their infants baptized then essentially raised their children unchurched, or situations where people have been baptized in another Christian denomination and now want to become Catholic.

Candidates go through most of the process with catechumens, but there are some alterations to the rites to properly accommodate them. Please consult the *Rite* for suggestions and guidelines. The significant difference between catechumens and candidates is recognized as they near the time of the Easter Vigil: Candidates must be prepared for and celebrate the sacrament of penance and reconciliation while catechumens are preparing for baptism. Candidates will not take part in the baptismal portion of the Mass of the Easter Vigil, but are called forward to join the others at the time of confirmation and for receiving the Eucharist.

Because it is neither possible nor desirable to always and everywhere follow a rigid and uniform schedule and guidelines for everything, the RCIA process is flexible to times and circumstances. Thus the skeletal sketch of timetables, and even of rites, which are contained herein is flexible. This is the "ideal" timetable, however, and these are the most significant rites of the *Rite of Christian Initiation of Adults.* Again, consult the *Rite* itself for other suggestions and guidelines.

Within each rite there are options which allow for making the rite appropriate for those involved in a particular ceremony.

THE RITE OF ACCEPTANCE INTO THE ORDER OF CATECHUMENS

The ritual for this first public rite of the RCIA program is easily recognized. The petitioners—inquirers who seek to become catechumens—stand outside the church building or outside of the main body of the church, knocking, asking admittance. Their sponsors are with them, to vouch for their sincerity. The priest or deacon goes to them, and each is called by name and asked, "What do you ask of God's Church?"; to which is answered: "Faith." Then, "What does faith offer you?"; to which is answered: "Eternal life." After this a series of statements of faith is publicly accepted by the petitioners, their sponsors publicly attest to their readiness to undertake the catechumenate, and the cross is signed on each forehead by the celebrant and by his or her respective sponsor. The cross may then be signed on the ears, eyes, lips, heart, shoulders, hands, and feet, each with appropriate words of blessing. *Receive the sign of the cross over your heart, that Christ may dwell there by faith.*[1]

Following a final blessing prayer, the celebrant leads the new catechumens and candidates, and their sponsors, into the church for the Liturgy of the Word as the assembly sings a psalm or appropriate hymn of welcome. After the readings and homily, it is customary to present the catechumens and candidates with a Bible and a small cross or crucifix. Intercessory prayers are then offered for them and the celebrant prays over them. Catechumens, with their sponsors and catechists, are usually dismissed for "breaking open the Word"—time spent in exploring and discussing the Scripture passages of the Sunday and how they apply to their lives—before the Liturgy of the Eucharist begins. *God our Father, help us to hear your Son. Enlighten us with your word, that we may find the way to your glory.²* The period known as the catechumenate has begun.

THE ROOTS AND WINGS OF THE RCIA

The *Rite of Christian Initiation of Adults* is still something of a mystery to many "cradle" Catholics. We know this has taken the place, so to speak, of "convert classes"; but why? And why all these extra rites that the whole parish is supposed to participate in? What do they mean, and how do they involve us?

The RCIA—often called the catechumenate—was universally revived following the Second Vatican Council and promulgated for the English-speaking Church in 1974, although the process had begun as early as the mid-1940's in the African Church. The *Rite* that is currently followed in the United States became mandatory in 1988. It is our adaptation of Christian initiation as it was practiced in the early centuries of the Church.

Becoming a Christian before the Constantinian reform (in 313) was a *very* serious move indeed, so the young Church insisted on an initiation process that practically guaranteed the new member would be faithful unto death itself. While our current RCIA process generally takes about a year, those first catechumens readied themselves for three or more years before they were baptized into the Church community. And while the parish community gives some support to the catechumens, particularly as sponsors and catechists, the early church community immersed itself in making the journey of faith with each and every prospective new member throughout that whole process of initiation.

The RCIA is rightly called a process, rather than a program—although it follows a systematically structured set of guidelines—because a person's journey of faith is a *lifelong* journey. The one who is seeking entry into the Catholic Church is beginning a portion of that journey with the guidance and support of catechists, sponsors, and the parish faith community in the hope that the Church will provide the best environment for that faith and relationship with God to grow and mature. And becoming a Catholic Christian in these early days of the twenty-first century is *still* a very serious move. It may be the *most* serious move a person will ever make in life, a fact that born-and-raised Catholics often do not have the proper appreciation for. This is our faith, but if

that faith is not freely and consciously *chosen,* the implications of it are not impacting our very way of life at every step. *Lord, protect your people always, that they may be free from every evil and serve you with all their hearts.*[3]

Thus does the Church give us the season of Lent. It is during Lent that we most seriously focus on our gift of faith through renewed prayer and fasting and almsgiving. *Father, you have taught us to overcome our sins by prayer, fasting and works of mercy. When we are discouraged by our weakness, give us confidence in your love.*[4] This is also the most intense part of the catechumen's journey. In fact, on the first Sunday of Lent, following the Rite of Election (see p. 14), catechumens become known as "the elect." And when the elect are baptized and received into the Church at the Easter Vigil on Holy Saturday (see p. 22), all in the parish community renew their baptismal promises with the new members.

In the early Church, the forty days of Lent totally immersed the whole community in preparation for new life with these elect. The rituals of the catechumenate were celebrated with gusto by the people, who understood their significance, not only for the elect, but also in their own respective journeys of faith.

Today's Church has lost much of the richness of its heritage that is found in the signs and symbols of our faith. The significance of the rich symbolism we find in our churches is lost on our non-historic minds. Many of us mutter about the inconvenience of longer liturgies in order to accommodate rites that we know nothing about. We fail to understand or appreciate the journeys that have led the elect to this point, and many of us conscientiously stay away from the most significant Mass of the year—the Easter Vigil—because we've heard it lasts two or more hours.

THE RITE OF ENROLLMENT OR ELECTION

The signs and symbols of Lent begin, usually in the dead of winter, with ashes and the color purple. The ashes remind us of our insignificance and our mortality—our creatureliness. Do we hear the words? *Remember, man…remember, woman…you are dust and to dust you will return.*[5] Without God, we cease to exist. And so the cross is signed upon our foreheads with last year's palm branches, dried and shriveled and charred. Ashes to ashes…dust to dust…nothing to nothing. The color purple is somber and mournful—a funeral pall. Do we wrap ourselves in its unrelenting sadness? *Turn to us with mercy, Lord; we have sinned against you.*[6] Without God, we cannot live. So we are called to penitence in the same way as our ancient forebears were called to penitence—in sackcloth and ashes.

With Lent comes also the second major rite of the RCIA, the second step in the Christian initiation process. On the first Sunday of Lent, the Rite of Enrollment or Election marks a momentous change in the life of the catechumen. Called to the cathedral, for the first time encountering the larger Church and the bishop who shepherds the whole diocese, catechumens hear their names called out. They enter

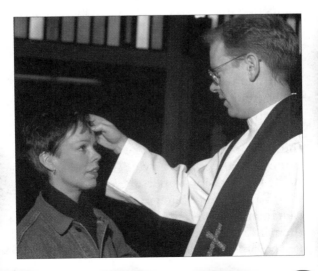

the cathedral's sanctuary with their sponsors, receive a special blessing from the bishop, and have their names enrolled in the Book of the Elect. From now until Holy Saturday, they are called "the elect" because they have been elected—initially sent forth by their respective parish communities and endorsed by their sponsors and their teachers, and ultimately elected by the *whole Church* in the persons of the bishop and the gathered assembly. This whole-Church acceptance has its foundation in faith on the election of God, for it is in God's name that the Church acts. The elect will walk the lenten road to Jerusalem with Jesus…die with him…so to enter new life, become a new creation, a Christian and a Catholic, in the new baptismal waters on Holy Saturday.

This transition from catechumen to elect is, in a sense, the most important transition in the process because it calls for a transformation in the person: a conversion of heart and mind, often a change of lifestyle. These elect have made the decision to persevere in their preparation and here publicly resolve to receive the sacraments of initiation into the Church. For them, the six weeks of Lent are known as the Period of Purification and Enlightenment.

THE RITE OF THE SCRUTINIES

On the third Sunday of Lent, the first Scrutiny is celebrated. The recommendation is to use the Lectionary readings from Cycle A for all the Scrutinies. The first one, then, flows out of the story of the Samaritan woman—*The water I shall give will become…a spring of…eternal life*[7]—and the intercessions for the elect on that day focus on that gospel message.

That, like the woman of Samaria, our elect may review their lives before Christ and acknowledge their sins, let us pray to the Lord....[8] The intercessions are followed by prayers of exorcism. *Free them from the slavery of sin, and for Satan's crushing yoke exchange the gentle yoke of Jesus.*[9] Then, as usual, the elect are dismissed for further reflection on the Scriptures before the rest of the assembly celebrates the Liturgy of the Eucharist.

This ritual is similarly repeated on the fourth and fifth Sundays of Lent. The second Scrutiny, on the fourth Sunday, relies on the story of the man born blind. *[The man who was blind] went and washed, and came back able to see.*[10] We pray: *That God may dispel the darkness and be the light that shines in the hearts of our elect...*[11] and the prayers of exorcism follow. *Free these elect from the false values that surround and blind them. Set them firmly in your truth, children of the light for ever.*[12]

On the fifth Sunday of Lent, we hear the story of the raising of Lazarus and celebrate the third Scrutiny. *I am the resurrection and the life.*[13] In our intercessions, we pray for the elect, and for ourselves and our world. *That the example and prayers of catechumens who have shed their blood for Christ may encourage these elect in their hope of eternal life.... That we too at Easter may again be confirmed in our hope of rising to life with Christ.... That the whole world, which God has created in love, may flower in faith and charity and so receive new life....* [14]The celebrant exorcises: *Free from the grasp of death those who await your life-giving sacraments and deliver them from the spirit of corruption.*[15]

During the third week of Lent, but not within the Sunday liturgy where the first Scrutiny is celebrated, the elect receive the first of two Presentations. For this Presentation of the Creed, readings are prescribed: *Hear, O Israel!... You shall love the LORD, your God, with all your heart....If you confess with your mouth that Jesus is Lord and believe in your heart that God raised him from the dead, you will be saved....upon this rock I will build my Church....*[16] As the Creed is presented to the elect, the assembly of the faithful recite it. The celebrant prays over the elect before their usual dismissal: *Purify them and make them...worthy to receive the grace of baptism.*[17]

During the fifth week of Lent, but not within the Sunday liturgy where the third Scrutiny is celebrated, the elect receive the Presentation of the Lord's Prayer. The prescribed readings for this ritual speak of God's parental love. *I have led you with cords of love.... You have received the Spirit that makes you God's children....Our Father, who art in heaven....*[18] The elect are called forward to listen to the gospel as it is proclaimed. The assembly is

invited to pray over the elect following the homily, then the celebrant prays over them—*Deepen the faith and understanding of these elect, chosen for baptism*[19]—and dismisses them for a further breaking open of the Word.

THE SACRAMENTS OF INITIATION

The third step in the RCIA is the long-awaited initiation of the elect into the Church. At the Easter Vigil, after dusk on Holy Saturday in anticipation the holiest day of the liturgical year—Easter Sunday—the long preparation is rewarded: the elect become "neophytes," brand

new Catholic Christians. The signs and symbols of this majestic liturgy begin outside the church doors, or at least outside the main body of the church—much as the journey of these joyful new members began outside the doors so many months ago. A new fire must be lit, from which to light a new paschal candle that will later be plunged into the new baptismal waters. *Christ yesterday and today, the beginning and the end, Alpha and Omega. All time belongs to him, and all the ages.*[20] Everything is new this night, clean and fresh and pure. *Christ our light.*[21] Even *we* feel new—aglow and basking in the warmth of this new Light of Christ. *Thanks be to God.*[22]

BAPTISM

First, of course, is baptism—that sacrament through which we become Christ's, and part of the communal body of Christ. The ritual of baptism begins with a Litany of the Saints which incorporates those saints whose names the initiates will be taking this night. Then the water is blessed. The new paschal candle is plunged into the baptismal pool or font as the celebrant prays for the coming of the Holy Spirit upon the waters, and that *all who are buried with*

Christ in the death of baptism rise also with him to newness of life.[23] And the people respond: *Springs of water, bless the Lord. Give him glory and praise for ever.*[24] The initiates then do the Renunciation of Sin, followed by the Profession of Faith. And then the immersion or pouring of the blessed waters. *I baptize you in the name of the Father...and of the Son...and of the Holy Spirit.*[25]

Because confirmation follows baptism in the initiation rites, there is no anointing with chrism during the baptism itself. The newly baptized is clothed in a white garment by his or her sponsors/godparents—*You have become a new creation and have clothed yourself in Christ*[26]—and then is presented a baptismal candle that has been lighted from the paschal candle—*You have been enlightened by Christ. Walk always as a child of the light and keep the flame of faith alive in your heart.*[27]

CONFIRMATION

A brief introduction to confirmation is followed by a short prayer silently uttered by the assembled community. The celebrant then stretches out his hands over the heads of the candidates in the blessing called the Laying on

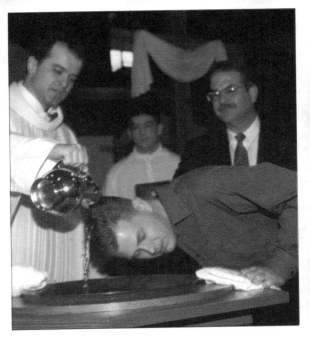

of Hands. *All-powerful God....Send your Holy Spirit upon them to be their helper and guide.*[28] Now each candidate individually, along with his or her sponsors/godparents, presents him or herself before the celebrant for the Anointing with Chrism. The sponsor's right hand is on the candidate's right shoulder as the sponsor gives the candidate's name to the confirming minister. Signing each forehead with the chrism, the celebrant repeats the name and confirms the person. *Be sealed with the gift of the Holy Spirit....Peace be with you.*[29] And the confirmand responds: *And also with you.*[30]

A Renewal of Baptismal Vows follows for the entire assembled community, and then the Sprinkling with Baptismal Water. *God...has given us a new birth by water and the Holy Spirit and forgiven all our sins. May he also keep us faithful to our Lord Jesus Christ for ever and ever.*[31]

EUCHARIST

The Prayers of the Faithful are now said, with the neophytes fully joining in as members of this particular church and the Church universal. The neophytes are also the ones who present the gifts at the altar this night. Then, following the Eucharistic Prayer, they are invited to receive the sacred body and blood of Christ for the first time. *This is the Lamb of God, who takes away the sins of the world.*[32] They may be joined in this joyful procession to the altar of the Lord by their sponsors/godparents, catechists, spouses, parents, sometimes even children. *Christ has become our paschal sacrifice; let us feast with the unleavened bread of sincerity and truth, alleluia.*[33]

THE SEASON OF EASTER

While the rites of the RCIA are now completed, the process is not. The new Catholic Christians continue to assemble with their catechists, and indeed with the whole parish community, throughout the season of Easter for a period of postbaptismal catechesis which is called "mystagogy," meaning "mystery," or more accurately, further catechesis on what it means to enter and to partake in the paschal mystery of the suffering, death, and resurrection of our Lord—the *whole* Christian mystery that comprises the *whole* of our life and faith. During these fifty days, the Sunday liturgies should specially focus on the new members of the body of Christ, and the people of the parish should make every effort to extend themselves in welcoming their new sisters and brothers as family. The stories from the Acts of the Apostles during the Easter season emphasize the community, and the continuing work of salvation through the ever-growing discipleship of the fledgling Church. This is the same emphasis that we wish to make in the Church of our times, for we are ordinary Christians entering into "ordinary time" in order to live the extraordinary lives of the baptized. *You are a chosen race, a royal priesthood, a holy people; praise God who called you out of darkness and into his marvelous light.*[34] ...*Go in the peace of Christ, alleluia, alleluia.*[35]

ENDNOTES

1. *Rite of Christian Initiation of Adults*, p. 59.
2. From the Opening Prayer for the Second Sunday of Lent. In *The Sacramentary*, p. 90.
3. From Solemn Blessing or Prayer Over the People for the Fifth Sunday of Lent. *Sacramentary*, p. 115.
4. From the Opening Prayer for the Third Sunday of Lent. *Sacramentary*, p. 98.
5. From the Giving of Ashes on Ash Wednesday. *Sacramentary*, p. 77.
6. From the Responsory on Ash Wednesday. *Sacramentary*, p. 78.
7. From the Gospel for the Third Sunday of Lent, Cycle A (John 4:5-42). In *Lectionary for the Mass, Second Typical Edition, Volume I.*
8. From Intercessions for the Elect for the First Scrutiny. *Rite*, p. 114.
9. From Exorcism for the First Scrutiny. *Rite*, p. 116.
10. From the Gospel for the Fourth Sunday of Lent, Cycle A (John 9:1-41). *Lectionary*.
11. From Intercessions for the Elect for the Second Scrutiny. *Rite*, p. 126.

12. From Exorcism for the Second Scrutiny. *Rite*, p. 127.

13. From the Gospel for the Fifth Sunday of Lent, Cycle A (John 11:1-45). *Lectionary*.

14. From Intercessions for the Elect for the Third Scrutiny. *Rite*, pp. 131.

15. From Exorcism for the Third Scrutiny. *Rite*, p. 133.

16. From Presentation of the Creed. *Rite*, p. 119. Quoted are excerpts from the First Reading (Deuteronomy 6:1-7); the Second Reading (Romans 10:8-13); and the Gospel (Matthew 16:13-18) for the Presentation of the Creed, No. 748, *Lectionary, Volume IV.*

17. From Prayer Over the Elect for the Presentation of the Creed. *Rite*, p. 122.

18. From Presentation of the Lord's Prayer. *Rite*, p. 135. Quoted are excerpts from the First Reading (Hosea 11:l,3-4,8e-9); the Second Reading (Romans 8:14-17,26-27); and the Gospel (Matthew 6:9-13).

19. From Prayer Over the Elect for the Presentation of the Lord's Prayer. *Rite*, p. 137.

20. From Preparation of the Candle for The Easter Vigil. *Sacramentary*, p. 172.

21. From the Procession for The Easter Vigil. *Sacramentary*, p. 173.

22. *Ibid.*
23. From Blessing of Water for The Easter Vigil. *Sacramentary,* p. 202.
24. *Ibid.*
25. From Baptism. *Rite,* p. 207-208.
26. From Clothing With a Baptismal Garment. *Rite,* p. 161 or 209.
27. From Presentation of a Lighted Candle. *Rite,* p. 161 or 209.
28. From Laying on of Hands. *Rite,* p. 163.
29. From Anointing with Chrism. *Rite,* pp. 164 or 211.
30. *Ibid.*
31. From Sprinkling with Baptismal Water. *Rite,* p. 167.
32. From The Order of the Mass. *Sacramentary,* p. 564.
33. The Communion Antiphon for The Easter Vigil. *Sacramentary,* p. 206.
34. From Period of Postbaptismal Catechesis or Mystagogy. *Rite,* p. 168 as based on 1 Peter 2:9.
35. From the dismissal for The Easter Vigil. *Sacramentary,* p. 207.

PRAYER FOR THE RCIA

O God, we thank you for implanting the gift of faith in human hearts. We thank you for sending Jesus, your Son, as the fullness of your love. May his life and mission lead us to share in your divine life.

Today we ask you to bless in a special way all inquirers, catechumens, and candidates, who have generously responded to the invitation of Jesus: "Come, follow me." Help them to persevere in their journey of faith despite any difficulties. Bless all those who minister through the RCIA program so that, under the guidance of your Holy Spirit, they may lead others to a life of faith in Jesus Christ. Grant that all parishioners will take an active role in bringing new members into the Church. Call us all to a renewal of our faith, and inspire us all to be your light in the world.

Liguori

ONE LIGUORI DRIVE
LIGUORI MO 63057-9999
$1.95
Cover Design by Jodi Hendrickson
Cover Photo: Gene Plaisted, OSC

ISBN 0-7648-0910-5

5 0 1 9 5 >

9 780764 809101

13880